What About Girlz

During the Pandemic

S H A R O N Y. D A V I D S O N

authorHOUSE®

AuthorHouse™
1663 Liberty Drive
Bloomington, IN 47403
www.authorhouse.com
Phone: 833-262-8899

Published by AuthorHouse 03/13/2024

ISBN: 979-8-8230-2388-7 (sc)
ISBN: 979-8-8230-2387-0 (e)

Library of Congress Control Number: 2024905318

Print information available on the last page.

CONTENTS

CONTENTS

DEDICATION

This journal is dedicated to all girls who has been struggling during and after the Pandemic. Girls who feel all alone and feel like they have no one to talk to. Know you are not alone; God always send someone or a word to help guide you through your situations. *Always remember weeping may endure for the night, but joy cometh in the morning. Psalm 30:5 (KJV)*

ACKNOWLEDGMENTS

First and foremost, I would like to give thanks, praise & worship to my God, who is the head of my life and household. Without God, none of this would be possible. I thank God for all my trials and tribulations. Bringing me through every one of them, molding me into the woman he wants me to be. I thank you God for making me, looking down on me and saying this is my daughter and this is good. I thank you God for my family, watching over us, supplying all our needs. Without you God, I am nothing, I thank you for being patient with me and guiding me every step of the way.

I want to thank all the young ladies and women who shared their experiences during the pandemic and giving words of encouragement to lift and inspire girls: Sarai, Chase, Adrianna, Shaniya, Brianna, Jamia, Renee, Celeste, Joyce, Stephanie, Christina, Ashley, Katrice, Andrea, Alexandria, Sonya, Jessica, Tracey & Alicia. Your voice and presence in this Journal will inspire & encourage girls.

Thank you, mom, and dad, for being the parents you were to us, always there and never wavering in your love for us. To my children Ashley, Christina, and Marquis, my grandchildren Ashton and Rylee; I thank you for being my push and inspiration to keep moving forward. My siblings, Martin, and Sheila, thank you for always being there, we have a bond that many siblings wish they had. God bless and keep each of you.

WHAT ABOUT GIRLZ?

The COVID-19 Pandemic caught most of the world off guard. We all subsequently endured months of social isolation, quarantining, mask-wearing, various tests etc., which caused and unrest that was at times unbearable and anxiety that was seemingly unshakeable. Due to all of this, each of us has our own unique stories about this challenging time. Amid all our emotions of frustration and setbacks, the time also presented opportunities for self-evaluation and growth. It is undeniable that this season of Pandemic has caused the world trauma, and its effects to our society will be revealed and studied for years to come.

However, this journal called, "What About Girlz, During the Pandemic" can start the healing process as these brave young ladies boldly share their stories of how they have managed and coped with the COVID-19 Pandemic. They are survivors, and their stories encourage its readers that you are too. Thank God for the ministry of Evangelist Sharon Davidson, who selflessly leads the charge in empowering our next generation of girls through her mentorship and guidance towards their divine destiny. Enjoy, as these young QUEENS take us on their survival journey through the COVID-19 Pandemic.

Rev. G. Maurice McRae, Jr.,
Pastor-Teacher
Little Rock Baptist Church
Brownsville, N.Y.

Thank You to Sharon Davidson for capturing the voice of young women! Your ongoing commitment to girls through WAG (What About Girlz) makes the difference in so many young women's lives. Your love of God shines through! May the Lord continue to bless you and keep you as you use your gifts to change the lives and hearts of young women. You are a mighty woman of God!

Rev. Omotayo Cole Cineus,
Pastor, Mother, Educator

What can I say about Whataboutgirlz and Sharon? Sharon is indeed a woman of God. The way she talks, even the way she walks for the Lord. Sharon loves the Lord, and she gives her all to Him and His word and she really knows the word and she preaches the word in and out. I Love You very very much. You are indeed a wonderful woman of God!

Your cousin Rev. Ronell Savits!
Pastor
Apostolic House of Deliverance
Brooklyn, N.Y.

INTRODUCTION

To All My Sista Girlz,

Where we start is not where we end. God said, *He knew our beginning before our end.* There are many reasons this journey of helping and aiding girls and mothers began. I grew up with both parents in the household. They instilled good stable morals and values in my siblings and me. It was not always easy, but we made it and did it as a family. I am a single parent raising my children and I also try to instill the same morals and values in them that my parents instilled in me. As I watch my daughters, family members, girls in general grow into teenagers and develop into young adults, my heart goes out to them. It's so hard for teens these days. Society is so different and hard from when I was growing up. It seems like no one cares anymore. I mentor girls, talk to them, and listen to them. Most girls feel as though no one listens to them or understands them. They feel alone, not wanted, and not appreciated. We all are driving towards our goals with a whole lot of praying, while walking in faith. On our journey, it sometimes seems like we are in park, idling but not moving, trying to figure out our correct destination, but the fact is, only God knows.

> *He hath made everything beautiful in his time:*
> *also, he hath set the world in their heart, so that*

1

> *no man can find out the work that God maketh from the beginning to the end.*
> *Ecclesiastes 3:11(KJV)*

March 2020 changed all our lives some changes were positive, and some were negative. We all gained, and we all lost. We lost loved ones; schools closed and our New Normal began. Everyone was told to stay home and practice social distancing. COVID-19 invaded the world. Schools went online for virtual learning; the world was shutdown. We had to reevaluate our way of living and do things totally different.

To all the girls and young woman in the world, I know it has not been easy. Not being able to go to school, jobs and hang out with your friends is a lot to handle. Sometimes your parents get so caught up in trying to supply for their households they sometimes forget about the children. Sometimes parents forget to ask their children, "how is the pandemic affecting you, what are your thoughts and feelings about not being able to go to school, work or hanging out with your friends? Are you fine mentally and physically? What can I do to help you through the Pandemic?" Girls and young women please know that your parents love you, you are important to us and most of all your voice and opinion MATTERS! Please know that we are all in this together and with help, guidance, and love from one another we can, and we will GET THROUGH THIS!

Whataboutgirlz Journal is a place where you can write your thoughts, feelings, and most of all find inspiration and encouragement from girls and women who cares for you and understands what you are going through. Journaling helps us put our thoughts and feelings on paper. When we write things down, we bring a vision to life. Journals are keepsakes that we hold dear and keep to ourselves. When we write things down, we can always go back and read and see what we overcame and what we carried out over time.

We are on this Journey together and WAG is here for you. Daily, sit back, take the time out of your busy schedule to read, meditate and find inspiration and encouragement in yourself and the girls of WAG. Express your passions and thoughts through words, poetry, songs, and drawings. I pray WAG (Whataboutgirlz) Journal inspires you, encourages you and motivates you to be the best you can be.

I believe Whataboutgirlz is the beginning of a long-lasting journey and relationship. Where we will learn, grow, laugh, and cry together.

God says, *"I know the plans I have for you."* Let's walk together to find our purpose, our goals, and our reason for life. Let us buckle up and enjoy this journal and journey we call life, together.

Stay True to Yourself Always
Regardless of what you are
going through in life.
Always stay true to yourself.

All About Me

Name: _____

Birthdate: _____

Age: _____

Zodiac Sign: _____

Parents: _____

Siblings: _____

Pets: _____

School, College, Job: _____

Favorite Teacher: _____

Best Friends: _____

Favorite Movies: _____

Social Media: _____

_____

Sports & Hobbies: _____

_____

That is What Girls Are Made Of

Bra Size: _____

Panty Size: _____

Shirt Size: _____

Pant Size: _____

Dress Size: _____

Shoe Size: _____

<u>Fashion Galore</u>

Favorite Designers: _____

Favorite Sneakers: _____

Favorite Perfume: _____

Favorite Make-up: _____

Favorite Colors: _____

Favorite Foods: _____

Favorite Artists: _____

Favorite Movies: _____

What do I wake up for,

my purpose in life?

To live, love & to be free to be me!

Name: Sarai Angel

Age: 13
Grade: 8th Grade

School During the Pandemic

At the beginning of the pandemic, I thought it would go by in about a month or two, I thought it was just an exaggerated flu type thing. But no, it was not, it really changed my life for the better. We were out of school for over 3 months. We went back a month after the day we were supposed to come back, we ended coming back on September 8, 2020, well at least I did.

Since they had different types of schooling, we all went back on different days. I was supposed to do the type where you go to school a few days out of the week and the other day is virtual. At first, I just wanted to go to school, and sometimes I still do, but I didn't realize that the precautions they had were not really that good for my health.

Grades: My Grades are good, in Math I have a 90.19, in ELA I have a 100.17, In Science, I have a 93.25, In Social Studies I have a 99.94, and in P.E I have a 95.36. I really don't have a strategy that I use to help me. I just read the assignments and do the work. My work is not that easy, but I am still able to keep the grades that I have. A majority of my work is hard which is why some kids have trouble keeping up their grades because they don't know how to exactly do the work. The teachers don't give you as much help as you would in face-to-face learning.

Even though the pandemic put a huge stop on the world doesn't mean you cannot keep going. Yeah, it may be hard, but you must keep pushing to pursue what you want to do in life. Just keep up the good work and you will eventually get to pursue your dreams and goals.

Date ___/___/_____

My happiness begins with me....

_____

_____

_____

_____

_____

_____

_____

_____

_____

_____

W.A.G

Sharon Y. Davidson

Date ___/___/_____

No matter what lies ahead of you, God is already there.

_____

_____

_____

_____

_____

_____

_____

_____

_____

W.A.G

Date ___/___/_____

Always remember you are Braver than you believe Stronger & Smarter than you think!

_____

_____

_____

_____

_____

_____

_____

_____

_____

W.A.G

Sharon Y. Davidson

Date ___/___/_____

Your Body, Your Rules!

_____

_____

_____

_____

_____

_____

_____

_____

_____

W. A. G.

It's okay to cry when you're hurt.
But wash your face and get up off
the floor when you're done.

You don't belong down there.

Chase

Age 14
Grade 9th

When I think of 2020, I think about the countdown: 10,9,8,7,6,5,4,3,2,1

HAPPY NEW YEARRR!!!! We all remember that day on December 31, 2019, when we were either in Time Square watching the ball drops at home getting drunk or turned up celebrating or even at church ringing in the new year with some nice praise music and Jesus. We prepared our resolutions for 2020: NEW YEAR NEW ME, IT'S ME MYSELF AND I, IT'S TIME FOR A CHANGE OR EVEN IM GOING TO BE NICE TO PEOPLE. LIESSSS!!! This was going to be the year that we would have 20/20 vision. But little did this world know that they were in for a rude awakening.

Let's take it back to January 26, 2020; when we heard the BREAKING NEWS: Kobe Bryant and his daughter Gianna Bryant die in helicopter crash on the way to a basketball game. The world went silent for that day people were in shock as a five-time Laker championship winner dies at the side of his 13-year-old daughter Gianna Bryant living in the footsteps of her father. While the world mourns the death of this renowned basketball player. Just across the Pacific Ocean in China, the onslaught of the COVID -19 pandemic begins.

We all heard the Tik-Tok sound made back in March "Coronavirus is coming...where's your face mask...if windows open close it!!!!" by then it had been so bad that you needed more than a face mask, hand sanitizer, face shields, and most importantly STAY SIX FEET APART. Businesses all around the country had started to close. The streets were so that you would not even see traffic, but more importantly the world was so silent you could hear your own thoughts. With the global pandemic happening in the world, we kids were forced into a new world Online School or what we now know, and love ZOOM. With this pandemic shaping them into a new way of life the words "I CAN'T BREATHE" was heard all around from George Floyd a Black man choked to death in Minneapolis, Minnesota by the wrath of Officer #1087 or known to the world as Derek Chauvin.

For 8 minutes and 46 seconds George Floyd was pinned down on the ground by the police officers of the Minneapolis Police Department. Officer Derek Chauvin was the culprit in this horrible murder. "TO PROTECT AND SERVE" yeah right that is the promise each officer is given when in the line of service. But it should really say "TO PROTECT AND SERVE ~WHITE AMERICANS" our country has dug in hole into institutionalized racism, so it is time from every person of color voice to be heard. The time is now, and the cavalry has arrived BLACK LIVES MATTER!! Established In July 2013 three phenomenal Black women created a social media hashtag that became a birth of the movement with their names Alicia Garza, Patrisse Cullors, and Opal Tometi.

Date ___/___/_____

Stop worrying about things you cannot change & put them in GOD's hands. God will fix it!

_____

_____

_____

_____

_____

_____

_____

_____

_____

_____

W.A.G.

Date ___/___/_____

In all situations NO means NO!

_____

_____

_____

_____

_____

_____

_____

_____

_____

_____

W.A.G.

Date ___/___/_____

I Am Joy. I Am Love.

_____

_____

_____

_____

_____

_____

_____

_____

_____

Date ___/___/_____

Treat Yourself Like You Treat Your Best Friend!

_____

_____

_____

_____

_____

_____

_____

_____

_____

_____

W.A.G.

Date ___/___/_____

I Am Doing My Best & That Is Enough!

_____

_____

_____

_____

_____

_____

_____

_____

_____

W.A.G.

You are amazing!
Do not let anyone ever
make you feel you are not.
If someone does.... walk away.
You deserve better.

Adrianna Bailey

Age:16
11th Grade

My COVID-19-Journey

When COVID-19 started, I was confused, and I didn't know what to do. I was lost, worried, and thought that I would not be able to see my family. I thought that I wouldn't be able to socialize with them. When I found out about the impact of COVID-19, I was so scared, and I did not want to go outside. Just like that, my life changed in March 2020. The second half of my 9th grade year I was stuck at home and all I did was homework, watched TV and played on my phone. I was unable to see my grandmothers, my aunts, and other family members. I began to struggle during the second half of 9th grade because of this pandemic. My grades were not as good as I wanted them to be because I was stressed. In addition to all that I have already mentioned, then my dad got sick. He was never officially diagnosed with COVID-19 but based on the symptoms; the doctor informed us that my dad probably had COVID-19. The doctor did not want my dad to go to hospital, due to the number of COVID-19 cases at that time. My dad, my buddy, was sick. My dad is the one who helps me with my homework but when he got sick, I got depressed and began stressing a little more. However, I knew that all I had to do was to pray about it. So, l prayed and prayed because I knew God would answer my prayers.

Throughout this pandemic, other things happened such as several Black Lives Matter protests. When George Floyd was killed by white police officers, I was nervous and upset. I wondered why Black people, because of our skin color, must continue to deal with this type of racism. COVID-19 and racism at the same time and the fact that I was home all day was a lot and I was wondering what was going on in this world. I kept asking why was George Floyd murdered by the ones who were expected to protect us? I kept wondering why my people are still facing the same prejudices and injustices that happened years ago? So many Black people have suffered due to racism. Rosa Parks was unable to sit in front of the bus. Rev. Dr. Martin Luther King, Jr., was killed.

Also, during all of this, I was unable to go to Church. I am a teenager, but I love going to Church. Fortunately, we were able to have virtual services and I was glad that my Church decided to worship via Zoom. I like ZOOM and it has allowed me to be part of the Tech Team, but it does not replace Church. However, my own family and my Church family have learned how to fellowship by using Zoom. My family has celebrated my Sweet 16th, my grandmother Morris' birthday, and my Auntie T's birthday via ZOOM. We have done several drive-bys to the homes of several family members and friends, as well as made a Birthday dinner for my Grandma Bailey. We have distributed food, desserts, book bags, masks with the Church's logo on them, flowers, and other nice items to several people. Even in the midst of COVID-19 and all the sadness, my family and I have still managed to have many positive and fun moments. During this past summer, my mother, my dad, and I took several car rides just to get some fresh air and to be with each other. I have had an opportunity to still smile, and I thank God my family is well. Since March 2020 to March 2021, a year later, I am still trying to go out every day, wearing a mask, to get some fresh air. I have adjusted to this new way of life and remote learning. My 10th year grades are better because I learned to give my concerns over to God.

Well, let me end this way: during this experience, I got to spend a lot more time with my parents in the house and my family too. I am enjoying bonding with my parents. We had a lot of love for each other before the pandemic, during this pandemic and we will continue to have love for each other after this pandemic. Two encouraging thoughts I want to express: you must stay positive and be happy. Have courage and know that God is always by your side in this life, in happy times and even through the stressful time.

Date ___/___/_____

Beautiful Girl You Were Made to Do Hard Things So Believe in Yourself.

_____

_____

_____

_____

_____

_____

_____

_____

_____

_____

W.A.G.

Date ___/___/_____

When in doubt, remember you are the daughter of the king and fix your crown!

_____

_____

_____

_____

_____

_____

_____

_____

_____

W.A.G.

Sharon Y. Davidson

Date ___/___/_____

Live every day like it is your last day!

_____

_____

_____

_____

_____

_____

_____

_____

_____

_____

_____

Date ____/____/_____

Stop worrying. Trust my timing. I will never fail you. - GOD

_____

_____

_____

_____

_____

_____

_____

_____

_____

_____

W.A.G.

AMAZING

LOVING

STRONG

HAPPY

SELFLESS

GRACEFUL

That Is who you are!

Shaniya

Age 17
Grade 11

African American people have been overlooked for many years. Our works and success have not been appreciated. The Black Lives Matter movement gave African Americans a voice. HEY, WE MATTER TOOO, WE DESERVE JUSTICE HOW MANY SUPPOSE TO DIE. HOW MANY TIMES DO WE LOOK THE OTHER WAY, ENOUGH IS ENOUGH! Me personally I feel being African America have given me experience of feeling less than, feeling overlooked by "people of importance ". Black people have been killed for smoking cigarettes while Caucasians storms the capital and damage everything not one-shot dead. In the midst of a pandemic, having to stop my normal lifestyle has given me more time to explore the internet and the same thing is still happening cops are being inappropriate, overly aggressive, and just rude. Some police officers feel too superior. The riots and the marches are how we take actions to be Hurd, to be respected, to be understood, we want our people to receive justice to their murders we want our Business respected and honored. The pandemic gave me a chance to really spend time with my family, learn new subjects and just become a better person. I had a chance to just figure myself out like what's important to me and who I want to be in life.

Date ___/___/_____

Make the time to love & care for yourself!

_____

_____

_____

_____

_____

_____

_____

_____

_____

W.A.G.

Date ___/___/_____

Be grateful for everything you receive.

_____

_____

_____

_____

_____

_____

_____

_____

_____

_____

W.A.G.

Date ___/___/_____

The only validation you need is within you.

_____

_____

_____

_____

_____

_____

_____

_____

_____

W.A.G.

I Love Myself.

I Believe in Myself.

I Support Myself.

WHAT ABOUT ME?

Brianna Rose

Age:17
Senior

2019-2021 seemed to be the year of complete isolation and dread. Most, if not all Americans apprehended the possibility of losing a loved one over a virus that seemed obstinate. The media and news outlets in 2019 made it clear that the virus was not planning on stopping presently. Consciously, the virus would come to affect Americans in every way of life. For instance, my mom received a lengthy letter saying the terms and conditions of our next school year. Sadly, but surely all students in the Pa district had to do cyber school that year. Since I'm a communicative person, it stung to hear that we won't be able to join extra-curricular clubs and sports. "What a shame", I thought; our administration was taking away one of the most significant years of my high school experience. Although a selfish thought, I could not help but feel discouraged by commencing school online. Proudly, I view myself to be somewhat of an optimist, even at my lowest. Yes, I was not pleased with the outcome of covid 19; however, this was an opportunity to show colleges that I'm flexible and able to manage any settings launched at me. With that mindset, I passed all my classes with flying colors. This reinsured my intellectual confidence, as well as shaped me further as a person. It can get very depressing when all you see on a day-to-day basis is death numbers from an unknown virus. However, what I learned from this depressing year was to conquer the moment. We'll never get to change what has been done but we can always change the way we respond to the crisis. Take time and learn what you like about yourself and the people around you, focus on how great life truly is. Covid-19 was an opportunity to adapt to change, and grow your perspective on unsettled times. Now that I'm in my senior year, and ready as ever, I'm going to make this my final stamp of courage. I'm going to try my hardest and conquer all the opportunities given. "Hope is important because it can make the present moment less difficult to bear. If we believe that tomorrow will be better, we can bear hardship today." -Thich Nhat Hanh Move forward. Learn. Grow.

Date ___/___/_____

She Turned Her Cant's into Cans & Her Dreams into Plans....

_____

_____

_____

_____

_____

_____

_____

_____

_____

_____

_____

W.A.G.

Date ___/___/_____

I Deserve to be Proud of Myself!

_____

_____

_____

_____

_____

_____

_____

_____

_____

_____

W.A.G.

Date ___/___/_____

Be in charge of how you feel today & always choose happiness.

_____

_____

_____

_____

_____

_____

_____

_____

_____

_____

W.A.G.

You Are:

Beautiful	Ecclesiastes 3:11
Victorious	Romans 8:37
Enough	2 Corinthians 12:9
Strong	Philippians 4:13
Amazing	Psalms 139:14
Never Alone	Matthew 28:20
Chosen	1 Thessalonians 1:4
Always Loved	Romans 8:38
Capable	Mark 10:27
Created	Genesis 1:31

RELATIONSHIPS

Jamia

Age: 17
Grade: Senior

2020 showed me a lot of relationships were fake. People will use you and show you fake love. But, most of all I learned in 2020 that life is very special and should never be taken for granted. Also, you need to watch who you bring in your life because not everyone you come across is meant to be in your life or is there forever. I do not need friends or a boyfriend around me to be happy because all they do is be in your business, judge you and add on to the stress in my life. Family is not always who they say they are. I learned to love from a distance because family will hurt you worse than you think.

The best thing that came out of 2020 is that I came closer to God, because of God I got through my storms in 2020 and I am still getting through. I am grateful and thankful for having a caring, merciful, loving, and unconditional God. Trust and believe in God because if God can do it for me, I know he will do it for you!

Date ___/___/_____

Don't Compare Yourself to Others, Be Like the Sun & the Moon & Shine When it is Your Time.

_____

_____

_____

_____

_____

_____

_____

_____

_____

W.A.G.

Date ___/___/_____

You Go Girl. You Better Walk into that Room Like God Sent You in There!

_____

_____

_____

_____

_____

_____

_____

_____

_____

_____

W.A.G.

Date ___/___/_____

Don't Quit, Keep the Faith!

_____

_____

_____

_____

_____

_____

_____

_____

W.A.G.

When You Have a Friend That is Going Thru a Personal Storm.

Instead of Being a Weathergirl & Spreading the News.

Try Being an Umbrella & Cover Them with Love!

Inspirational Quote from Maya Angelou:

"I've learned that people will forget what you said, people will forget what you did, but people will never forget how you made them feel."

Feelings mean so much, they go deep and can stay with you forever we should always remember to treat people how we want to be treated and that will become so clear as you grow into being a woman.

Renee Savage

Good day my daughter. I want you to know that you are Special. You are the essence of your destiny. It's about how you see and perceive yourself. Know in life that there will be moments of sunshine and rain, but you will be able to withstand the storm. There is a rainbow. I want you to know that you are beautiful. I need you to develop your character, choose in life what you will hear and accept. Feed your mind, body, and spirit with words and songs of encouragement. Talk to yourself:

Sharon Y. Davidson

Mirror, Mirror on the wall I am:

B old
E xtraordinary
A wesome
T alented
U nique
I mpressive
F antastic
U nlimited
L ovely

**Every day is a new beginning so love and
nurture yourself. I am BEAUTIFUL**
*"Born again and free, a brand new me,
feeling free and loving me"*
Celeste Lucas Powers, LMSW

51

Date ____/____/_____

Girlz, God meets you where you are at, not where you pretend to be!

_____

_____

_____

_____

_____

_____

_____

_____

_____

_____

W.A.G

Date ___/___/_____

Girlz, make plans for your future. Tap into your passion!

_____

_____

_____

_____

_____

_____

_____

_____

_____

W.A.G.

Date ___/___/_____

REMINDER: YOU GOT THIS!!

_____

_____

_____

_____

_____

_____

_____

_____

_____

_____

W.A.G.

Be Happy & Remember Your Roots

Family is Everything!

WORDS OF INSPIRATION

Life is wonderful and not always easy, but we must always stay focused on what it is we have. Believe and trust that God is using you in a very special way to shine his light and share his love. May you always have an angel on your side.

God can and will bless you with everything you need - you will always have more than enough to do all kinds of good things for yourself, as well as others. You could be making a great and wonderful difference in someone's life by just being kind.

Remember to always stay focused and keep God first in your life - no matter what others do or say. Faith keeps you going...believe that each day is a gift from God.

Joyce Biggs

I Am Fighting So You Don't Have To!

I am fighting so you don't have to wear your curly coiled hair straight

I am fighting so you don't have to suffer from The Imposter Syndrome

I am fighting so you don't have to act like your PowerPoint Presentation is not the best one presented

I am fighting so you don't have to be afraid to say I don't know

I am fighting so you don't have to earn less than white men and women

I am fighting so you don't have to fight the same fights our great, great, great grandmothers fought

I am fighting so you don't have to think your opinion doesn't matter

I am fighting so you don't have to feel unprotected and undervalued

I Am Fighting So You Do Not Have To!

Stephanie Arno

Date ___/___/_____

Don't Just Dare to Dream. If you have a dream, make it your goal.

_____

_____

_____

_____

_____

_____

_____

_____

_____

_W. A. G._

Date ___/___/_____

Be careful what you think because your thoughts become reality.

_____

_____

_____

_____

_____

_____

_____

_____

_____

W.A.G.

Date ___/___/_____

Your intuition and gut feelings are your guardian angels. Trust them!

_____

_____

_____

_____

_____

_____

_____

_____

_____

_____

W.A.G.

Date ___/___/_____

Girlz; do not let your heart grow cold because someone mishandled you. Shake it off and move on.

_____

_____

_____

_____

_____

_____

_____

_____

_____

_____

W.A.G.

Sharon Y. Davidson

Date ___/___/_____

Shine bright like a diamond so the world can see you!

_____

_____

_____

_____

_____

_____

_____

_____

_____

_____

W.A.G.

Nobody's Perfect.

That is Why Pencils Have Erasers!

WHAT MAKES YOU HAPPY?

The pandemic was a very unexpected period. People lost their homes, jobs, and their loved ones. Though many tragic things have transpired, many positive things have come about. Many people were able to start businesses, become successful and start doing the things that truly makes them happy! I've learned life is what you make it. Any situation can be a negative if you only think of the bad in it. Start thinking about the positive things in life and situations and more positivity will come to you. Many were able to change their lives during the pandemic by staying positive and focusing on what is important to them. Take the time to find out what makes you happy, what goals you want to accomplish. Start to journal, write down your affirmations. Write down what you are thankful and grateful for and write down your goals.

James 1: 2-4 "Dear brothers and sisters, when troubles of any kind come your way, consider it an opportunity for great joy. For you know that when your faith is tested, your endurance has a chance to grow. So let it grow, for when your endurance is fully developed, you will be perfect and complete, needing nothing."

Christina Smith-Craig

Hey beautiful,

If I had to leave you with anything, I would say "love on you." Loving on you is the foundation for today and tomorrow. When you learn to love you, you teach others how to love and treat you. When you learn to love you, you learn to believe in you and truly believing in you opens the door to endless opportunities. Learning to love me taught me how to say no to things that did not serve me. Learning to love me made me go for that job even though fear tried to tell me not to. Most importantly learning to love me gave me the strength to truly trust God's will for my life.

Alexandria Johnson

Sharon Y. Davidson

Date ___/___/_____

Fill your free time with someone who is worthy of it, not just a space filler.

_____

_____

_____

_____

_____

_____

_____

_____

_____

_____

W. A. G.

Date ___/___/_____

Hold Your Head Up High Because You Did Not Quit!

_____

_____

_____

_____

_____

_____

_____

_____

_____

_____

W.A.G.

Date ___/___/_____

Hello Beautiful, today is a wonderful day because you are here!

_____

_____

_____

_____

_____

_____

_____

_____

_____

_____

W.A.G.

Are you dealing with anxiety,
depression & low esteem?

We all are, don't suffer in silence.

Don't be afraid to ask for help.
We all need each other!

I don't know about you girlsssss but as soon as that lockdown happened, I started panicking! Me being the woman I am, I love to keep my hair, nails & toes done! The first thing I started thinking about was the fact that I can fix my hair but what would I do about my nails and toes?! This is when I realized I would really put my Amazon prime membership to use (as if I didn't order stuff everyday prior lol). When I tell you I started ordering everything under the sun for nails! Everything that I would see my nail tech use I added to my cart! When my order came, I didn't know what to do with it BUT I was determined to figure it out! I started practicing on myself, my mom & sister and babyyyyyyyy did I suck?! But we rocked them, and I kept practicing! I started to enjoy doing nails and became infatuated with doing them! I enrolled in a beginner nail tech class with a local nail tech & that changed my whole mindset. Once I completed the class it was over from there, I went full force on my nail journey, I started practicing on all my friends and family. My job laid me off and from that moment on I decided I would go full speed and master doing nails. I eventually signed up for a second beginner nail tech class because as easy as it looked, it really was not that simple! The second class boosted my confidence even more! A few months later I decided I wanted to make a living out of doing nails, my options were to either find a job that I can potentially get laid off from again or find a way to be my own boss. I made my decision, and I made the biggest investment in myself that I've ever had! I enrolled in a Nail Technology program to obtain my state license! This commitment was not easy with me being a mom, significant other & having to run a household BUT I did it! I now run a successful business that is flourishing daily! I am so grateful for my support system; I thank God for making this opportunity possible. I want you young ladies to know that you can do ANYTHING you put your mind to! If college is for you go for it! If a trade is for you go for it! There is no right or wrong way to mold your future! The ONLY wrong way is doing what everyone else wants you to do and not what YOU want! You will love everyday much more when you're doing what you love daily! Feel free to follow my social media and reach out to me for any pointers on how to become a nail tech IG: @itsthenailsforme_

Sincerely,
Your Fairy Nail Mother
Ashley Stephens

Sharon Y. Davidson

Date ___/___/_____

Stay Positive!

_____

_____

_____

_____

_____

_____

_____

_____

_____

_____

Date ___/___/_____

If you can feel it, you can heal from it. Don't ignore your feelings. Acknowledge & get help.

_____

_____

_____

_____

_____

_____

_____

_____

_____

_____

W.A.G.

I AM COURAGEOUSLY
IMPERFECT.

I AM BEAUTIFULLY BROKEN.

STILL, I AM AN
UNSTOPPABLE FORCE.

"ALWAYS" IS THE ANSWER"

I used to LOVE math. Problem solving, equations, factions…it was my whole vibe. But when I got into the 11th grade, everything changed. My algebra teacher, Mr. Baldwin, was a very quiet man that didn't appear to have a love for shaping young minds. He loved chaos. In fact, let's only refer to him as "Bane" from the Batman movie moving forward.

One semester, Mr. Bane introduced a new concept that ultimately caused me to hate the subject altogether: algebraic expressions. Now, without completely boring you with all the details, he would ask the class mathematical phrases/sentences that had to be answered with one of the following words: always, sometimes, or never. No matter how much I studied, I could never get these questions right! And to make matters worse, he explained the concept poorly and wouldn't answer our questions thoroughly. I ended up having to take night school and summer classes just to graduate on time, largely due to the grade I'd gotten in his class! Ugh. Have you ever had a horrible teacher that made you hate a subject you loved? If so, I'm sorry sis. Ugh!!!

In thinking about Mr. Bane's class recently, I reflected on those mathematical phrases differently. This time, I thought of those statements regarding a few relationships that have been very difficult for me this year. I don't know about you but sometimes, I have full-out arguments with people in my head, based on conversations we may or may not have ever had! Sometimes, my whole mood shifts because of these battles that play out in my mind and I often "leave" feeling like that person "always" refuses to take accountability for their actions. Or, that they "never" listen and that "sometimes," I feel like I'd be better off never talking to them again! But let's go a step further.

I also look at my life as a single woman with no children and think I'll "never" find love. Or that "sometimes" I just do not believe I'm enough...pretty enough, small enough, tall enough, good enough...have you ever been there? And it gets extra complicated when the feeds on my social media accounts are filled with engagements and announcements! I often wrestle between what is true and what is a big, fat, lie. Maybe you've struggled with that too...

Nevertheless, all I know is this. At the end of the day, I ultimately have everything I need and will "ALWAYS" be loved. I am loved when I get everything right and when I fall short. I love it when my eyebrows look shady and when I've got a GOOD beat. I am loved when my nails are chipped and when I've got a fresh pedi. I am loved when I feel alone and afraid, and when I am surrounded by friends and family. I am ALWAYS loved. In this case, that is the correct answer. So, when you get carried away in your thought-life by the harsh realities of life or false evidence that appears to be real, when it comes down to it, one thing is sure. At every point, in every season, just as you are - - you will always be loved by God.

Katrice Walker

Date ___/___/_____

Fall in love with someone who wants you and waits for you. Someone who understands you in good times and in bad times.

_____

_____

_____

_____

_____

_____

_____

_____

W.A.G.

Date ___/___/_____

You don't meet people by accident. There is always a reason, a blessing, and a lesson.

_____

_____

_____

_____

_____

_____

_____

_____

_____

_____

W.A.G.

Date ___/___/_____

There is always a light at the end of the tunnel. KEEP PUSHING QUEEN!

_____

_____

_____

_____

_____

_____

_____

_____

_____

_____

_____

W.A.G.

Sharon Y. Davidson

Date ____/____/_____

Girlz, Sit Back & Relax. God, has you covered!

_____

_____

_____

_____

_____

_____

_____

_____

_____

_____

_____

W.A.G.

Believe in...

- How beautiful you are

- How capable you are

- Your high potential

- Your hidden talents

- The Power within you

- Everything you will do

- The future you

- Your dreams coming true

Inherent in the seed of the tree is the tree

Fall is here, and acorns are falling from oak trees into yards everywhere. Acorns can be grown into oak trees, if properly handled. It's amazing that an acorn is about 2" long but can grow into a mature live oak that stands between 60 and 100 feet tall!

When you see an acorn (or any seed for that matter), you are looking at possibility. The tree is in there, but it must be cared for before it becomes an oak tree. The same applies to you. Inherent in you is something greater than what you see or believe in yourself. God has placed a purpose in you and the only way it will grow is if that purpose is handled properly. Find time to journal regularly and learn about yourself. Study God's word and ask Him to show you what your purpose is. You may not find out right away but stay in the Word and the Word will speak to you. An oak tree takes 15-20 years to mature but it won't mature if it is not watered. You are beautiful. You are known. You are loved. What is inherent in you?

Andrea Harrison

A letter to the young girls and young ladies who are my sisters.

You were perfectly created and designed.

You were perfectly sculpted and chiseled into the image that God saw fit for you. You were created with love. God hand crafted your beautiful soul and spirit.

God also created you to do and be the best you, you can be, no matter what. Please believe it. You are awesome.

Remember you are here for a reason, you have a purpose, a DeVine purpose please my sisters fulfill your purpose, it is part of your life journey.

Know that you are worth it and deserves to be loved, no matter what you may face in life, know that it is only for a season and God is in it with you.

Most importantly love God your creator, love yourself and love others.

God bless you
Sincerely Ms. Sonya McCray

Date ____/____/_____

Hey Girl! You are beautiful inside & out!

_____

_____

_____

_____

_____

_____

_____

_____

_____

W.A.G.

Date ___/___/_____

It's easy to stand with the crowd. It takes courage to stand alone!

_____

_____

_____

_____

_____

_____

_____

_____

_____

_____

W. A. G.

Date ___/___/_____

There is always tomorrow to get it right!

_____

_____

_____

_____

_____

_____

_____

_____

_____

W.A.G.

Not Just This Day, But Every Day.

> ➤ Be Strong

> ➤ Be Bold

> ➤ Be Independent

> ➤ Be Passionate

Young ladies we are so much more than we think of ourselves our body is a temple, but society makes it feel mental what they see is not what they get say it loud

"I am more"

I am full of creativity electricity runs through me

I am alive and as long as I am alive

I will survive the pandemic only show me what I have inside my body is a temple beautiful and wise

I have survived!

My Name is Jessica Instagram @glammed_byjess

I am a hair stylist from NY. I recently moved to Atlanta. I almost lost my passion because working with people is not easy. But God will use people to speak life into you. My hands are a blessing from God I want to use them to change people. As I am depending on his word, He may use me to point people to him. A true transformation of life!

Jessica Thompson

Great day my beautiful girls, young ladies, and young women. I say great day because you it to be just that great and nothing other. We wake up each day knowing that God has brought us through another night. We are thankful, so we must speak powerful phrases over our days during our life to uplift and encourage one another.

I want to introduce myself; my name is Tracey Whitehead. I am a hardworking mother, sister, and friend. I worked for the NYPD for 28 years. My son is the proud CEO of PTG365, an amazing car business, and the 1st millionaire in my family. My son gave me the PTGMOM name after starting his business, our first powerful phrase is "Mind Over Matter." Your mind controls!

Tracey Whitehead

Sharon Y. Davidson

Date ___/___/_____

Girlz, don't let them take anything from you but notes!

_____

_____

_____

_____

_____

_____

_____

_____

_____

W.A.G.

Date ___/___/_____

YOU PRAYED FOR IT; NOW GO GET WHAT YOU PRAYED FOR!

_____

_____

_____

_____

_____

_____

_____

_____

_____

_____

W.A.G.

Date ___/___/_____

God made you different, don't ruin it trying to be like everybody else!

_____

_____

_____

_____

_____

_____

_____

_____

_____

W.A.G.

I praise you because I am fearfully and wonderfully
made; your works are wonderful, I know
that full well. (Psalm 139:14 – NIV)
Beautiful (Outside and Inside)
Rev. Alicia Bailey

Breaking News For All Young Ladies! You are so beautiful! Let me repeat it again: You are so beautiful. You are not only beautiful on the outside, but you are beautiful on the inside. Do you believe those words? I hope you do because God has created you in His image! Because God is the author and finisher of our lives, let me sound the trumpet that "you are "fearfully and wonderfully made; your works are wonderful, and I know that full well." Every morning, when you wake up, you should declare that you are so special, gifted, talented, smart, awesome, and unique. It does not matter the color of your skin or whether you have pimples or the perfect skin texture, you are beautiful! It does not matter how much you weigh, your hair type, or your height (short or tall), you are destined for wonderful things. It does not matter if you live in an apartment, house, or shelter; you are a winner. It does not matter whether your family is rich or poor, you are still beautiful. It does not matter if you have a lot of clothes, shoes, sneakers, or jewelry, you're here to fulfill your purpose. You are a Princess developing into a Queen. You are an original and nobody can imitate you.

God wants you to be your best because you were born to shine, to stand tall, to soar like an eagle, and to rise above the highest mountain. Nothing is impossible for you to

achieve because you are called to make a difference. You
have the ability to do all things through Christ; so please
do not allow fear, peer pressure, your haters, negativity,
or anyone to keep you from smiling. Do you understand
that you are so blessed, gorgeous, and precious in God's
sight? You are the next Author, Doctor, Nurse, Teacher,
Professor, Pastor, Minister, Business Owner, Psychologist,
Actress, Chef, Lawyer, Athlete, Guidance Counselor, or
any profession you wish to pursue. Never underestimate
your worth and your beauty. You are more than a conqueror.
You are a beautiful daughter of the Most High God and
you are part of His Royal Court. God is about to bless
you mightily. Get Ready, Get Set, and Go! Make all your
dreams come true. Do not compromise your beauty just to
be popular. Stay true to yourself! Love yourself and shout
"I am Beautiful--Outside and Inside!"

MAKE YOUR GOALS SMART

Setting goals can be a wonderful way to challenge yourself to make healthy lifestyle change. Set yourself up for success by making your goals SMART!

Make goals in your life to help you become the person you want to be. Make goals that you know you can achieve. Goals help you set standards in your life and keep you moving towards your dreams. DREAM BIG & TAP INTO YOUR FUTURE!

Specific = What is your goal?

Measurable = How will you keep track of your progress?

Attainable = How will you achieve your goal? Make a plan!

Relevant = How will this goal help you?

Timely = When will you achieve your goal?

S My Goal is:

M I will track my progress by:

**A I will achieve this goal by doing
the following:**

R This goal helps me because:

**T I will complete this goal by
(date):**

MY HELP MATE

The Bible has many verses that are inspirational & motivational, reminding us that God is always with us. These passages are helpful to remember whenever you find yourself going through doubt and uncertainty.

Deuteronomy 31:6 "Be strong and courageous, do not be afraid or tremble at them, for the LORD your God is the one who goes with you. He will not fail you or forsake you."

Psalm 23:4 "Even though I walk through the darkest valley, I will fear no evil, for you are with me; your rod and your staff, they comfort me."

Psalm 34:10 "Those who seek the LORD lack no good thing."

Psalm 55:22 "Cast your cares on the LORD and he will sustain you; he will never let the righteous be shaken."

Isaiah 41:10 "'Do not fear, for I am with you; Do not anxiously look about you, for I am your God. I will strengthen you, surely, I will help you, Surely I will uphold you with My righteous right hand.'"

Isaiah 49:13 "Shout for joy, you heavens; rejoice, you earth; burst into song, you mountains! For the LORD comforts his people and will have compassion on his afflicted ones."

Zephaniah 3:17 "The LORD your God is with you, the Mighty Warrior who saves. He will take great delight in you; in his love he will no longer rebuke you, but will rejoice over you with singing."

Matthew 11:28-30 "'If you are tired from carrying heavy burdens, come to me and I will give you rest. Take the yoke I give you. Put it on your shoulders and learn from me. I am gentle and humble, and you will find rest. This yoke is easy to bear, and this burden is light.'"

14:1-4 "'Don't let your hearts be troubled. Trust in God, and trust also in me. There is more than enough room in my Father's home. If this were not so, would I have told you that I am going to prepare a place for you? When everything is ready, I will come and get you, so that you will always be with me where I am. And you know the way to where I am going.'"

Isaiah 40:31 "Those who hope in the LORD will renew their strength. They will soar on wings like eagles; they will run and not grow weary, they will walk and not be faint."

1 Corinthians 10:13 "The temptations in your life are no different from what others experience. And God is faithful. He will not allow the temptation to be more than you can stand. When you are tempted, he will show you a way out so that you can endure."

2 Corinthians 4:16-18 "Therefore we do not lose heart. Though outwardly we are wasting away, yet inwardly we are being renewed day by day. For our light and momentary troubles are achieving for us an eternal glory that far outweighs them all. So we fix our eyes not on what is seen, but on what is unseen, since what is seen is temporary, but what is unseen is eternal."

Philippians 4:6-7 "Do not be anxious about anything, but in every situation, by prayer and petition, with thanksgiving, present your requests to God. And the peace of God, which transcends all understanding, will guard your hearts and your minds in Christ Jesus."

Philippians 4:13 "I can do all this through him who gives me strength."

Joshua 1:9 "Be strong and courageous. Do not be afraid; do not be discouraged, for the LORD your God will be with you wherever you go."

W.A.G. Whataboutgirlz Pledge

I am fearfully and wonderfully made.

I am an expression of beauty, joy, and love.

I was created by my father who made me in his likeness.

I am the most important thing in the world to me.

I can do all things through Christ who strengthens me.

I am the light of the world.

I deserve the best.

I am ready to enjoy this thing called life and live it to the fullest.

I am a girl, and I am growing into a woman!

I pray this journal has made a positive change in your life. Hold your head up high and walk into your destiny!!!

To All My Girlz,

In a fast-ever-changing world, there is so much for you to do and to worry about. Staying focused and being the best you that you can be is what you strive for daily.

I pray this Journal is a blessing to you. I hope it inspires, encourages, and uplifts you. Please take the time to write to me letting me know how Whataboutgirlz Journal has affected your life also what areas of your life you are working on to become the best you can be.

To learn more about WAG- Whataboutgirlz please visit:
Instagram: @whataboutgirlz.org
Whataboutgilrz@gmail.com
www.whataboutgirlz.org
Facebook: W.A.G.-whataboutgirlz

MEET THE VISIONARY

Evangelist Sharon Davidson is a woman after God's own heart. Sharon is a mother, mentor, seminarian, and the founder of WAG- Whataboutgirlz Organization since 2003.

The WAG organization combines all her passions through offering ministry, mentoring, and coaching to young girls and women. Sharon takes pride in giving girls and women much needed information and attention which helps mold them into respectful, confident, and educated women of God. Sharon's commitment to all mankind is proven in her neighborhood and local community-based organizations. Sharon is a faithful member and part of the ministerial staff of St. John AME Church. She is the Christian Education Director, she has implemented a girl's mentoring program the Gems of Hope. Sharon Davidson is the proud mother of three children and two grandchildren.

Sharon's Motto Is, "If I can inspire one young lady & one family, I have done enough."

Printed in the United States
by Baker & Taylor Publisher Services